The Sweetness of His Love

Stories of 'Abdu'l-Bahá

The Sweetness of His Love
Stories of 'Abdu'l-Bahá

Written by Jacqueline Mehrabi · *Illustrated by Jaci Ayorinde*

BELLWOOD PRESS®

WILMETTE, ILLINOIS

Bellwood Press
401 Greenleaf Avenue, Wilmette, Illinois 60091
Copyright © 2021 by the National Spiritual Assembly of the Bahá'ís of the United States
All rights reserved. Published 2021
Printed in China on acid-free paper ∞

ISBN 978-1-61851-193-5

24 23 22 21   4 3 2 1

Illustrations by Jaci Ayorinde
Cover and book design by Patrick Falso

Contents

"Blessed, doubly blessed, is . . . the heart that hath tasted the sweetness of His love."

—Bahá'u'lláh

The Master

It was a warm sunny day in May and the garden was full of flowers. Birds swooped down to drink the clear water in the pool, feeling safe in this lovely garden where no one would harm them.

Inside the house servants were busy making the meal and visitors sat in comfortable cushions drinking lemonade and eating delicious sweets made of nuts and honey. This was a house where everyone was welcomed and no one was ever turned away.

The owner of the house was Bahá'u'lláh, Who worked at the court of the King of Persia. He was very kind and was known as "The Father of the Poor." Later, people learned that He had come with a new message of love from God that would bring peace to all the people in the world.

The day came to an end. Birds chirped quietly as they settled down in their nests. The people in the house finished their work and chanted prayers to thank God for all the good things that had happened during the day.

But the best thing of all was about to happen. As the clock struck midnight, a perfect baby boy was born in that happy home. His mother was the beautiful Navváb, and His father was Bahá'u'lláh.

The baby was named Abbás after His grandfather. Many years later, when He was grown up, He became known as 'Abdu'l-Bahá. But Bahá'u'lláh called Him "the Master," because He knew His son would grow up to be wise and holy.

School

A good man, called Nabíl, had sore eyes and was feeling very miserable. When the Master's mother, Navváb, heard about it she made some special ointment and sent it to him. When Nabíl put the ointment on his eyes they soon became better.

One day, Nabíl was taken by a friend to the house where Navváb lived. The first person he saw was the Master, who was then six years old. He was standing at the door of Bahá'u'lláh's room and smiled at Nabíl as he passed by.

Another day when Nabíl was visiting the house he met the Master's uncle, Kalím. Kalím said that the servant who usually took the Master to school had not returned from the market. So he asked Nabíl if he would take the little boy to school instead.

Nabíl was very pleased to do this. The Master came out of Bahá'u'lláh's room wearing a hat and a warm coat and walked down the steps to the gate. He held Nabíl's hand and they chatted as they walked along together.

When they reached the school the Master looked up at Nabíl and said: "Come again this afternoon and take me home." Nabíl promised he would and felt very happy as he hurried back to the house of Bahá'u'lláh.

The Sheep

One lovely day, the Master was enjoying riding His pony over the green fields and up the mountainside. He was on His way to visit some shepherds in the hills. The shepherds lived in a village owned by Bahá'u'lláh. All the houses, the fields, and the sheep belonged to Bahá'u'lláh too. The farmers grew the corn and looked after the animals, and Bahá'u'lláh gave them money, food, and medicine when they were ill. The farmers loved Bahá'u'lláh very much.

The Master was only seven years old, so a servant was looking after Him on His long ride to the hills. They soon saw the shepherds with the sheep. The servant told the Master that when the owner, or his son, came to visit the shepherds he should thank them for looking after the sheep by giving them a present.

The Master wondered what He could give, for He no food or money. Then He had a good idea and said, "I give to the shepherds some of the sheep in their flocks!"

The shepherds were very surprised at such a generous gift. Later, when Bahá'u'lláh heard what His Son had done, He was very pleased and said that one day the Master would give Himself away as well!

Illness

The children were playing in the garden. The Master was now eight, His sister Bahíyyih was six, and His little brother Mihdí was four. The Master had not been very well during the past year. The doctors said that He was going to die, and there was no medicine to make Him better.

But one day the Master became well again. The doctors were astonished and did not know how such a thing could have happened.

Many years later, when the Master was quite old, He told some of His friends this story. He said that there is always a reason why things happen. If He had been well He would have been staying in their country house, but because He was so ill He was with His family in their town house at a time when they needed His help. One day some men came and took His Father away. This upset the family and made them feel very worried. But the young Master was able to help His mother by running errands and helping look after His little brother and sister.

Hunger

Bahá'u'lláh had done nothing wrong. He had been put in prison just because He believed in the Báb, Who had brought a wonderful message from God. People broke into the family's beautiful house in Tehran and stole everything they could. They took away all the pictures, books, and ornaments; all the furniture, carpets, and toys.

The Holy Family had to run away. They lost all their belongings and had no money to buy food. One day, when the Master was very hungry, all His mother had to give Him was a small amount of dry flour, which she put in the palm of His hand.

The Chase

People who believed in the Báb's new message from God were called "Bábís." There were many of them living in the town where the Master lived. But there were other people who were very unfriendly to them.

Once a gang of boys tried to catch the Master. "Here is the Bábí!" they shouted, as they charged down the streets after Him. Other boys joined the chase, through dark alleys, around narrow corners, jumping and swerving down dirty roads.

The Master raced in front of them, tightly holding some money, tied in a handkerchief, in His hand. It was money His auntie had given Him for His mother to buy food for the family.

Most of the boys were bigger than He was. They nearly caught Him, but He ran into the entrance of a house and hid there until it was dark.

The boys stopped, not daring to go near the house. They waited until the Master came out, then threw stones after Him as He ran the rest of the way home.

Money

Navváb and her two youngest children were huddled together trying to keep warm. They were hungry for they had not eaten any food all day.

Bahá'u'lláh, the beloved husband of Navváb, was locked away in a dark prison, and the Holy Family were hiding in a small house. Most of the people in the town were too frightened to help them, so Navváb had sent the Master to His aunt's house to borrow some money for food.

The hours passed by, and the Master had not returned. The other children fell asleep, although their stomachs were empty, and Navváb was weak with worry.

Suddenly she heard the sound of feet. The door opened and the Master came into the room. Boys had been chasing Him all the way home and, too tired to speak, He gave the money to His mother and fell sound asleep on the floor.

The Gang

One day the Master was walking alone through the streets on His way home from the market. Looking over His shoulder, He saw a gang of boys running up behind Him. They raced toward Him throwing stones and shouting, "Bábí! Bábí!"

Although the Master was only a small boy at this time, He was very brave. The bullies came nearer and nearer. Suddenly, to their surprise, the Master turned around and rushed toward them!

They were so frightened that they turned and ran away as fast as their legs could carry them! And they never again called the Master names or threw stones at Him.

A Terrible Place

When Bahá'u'lláh was in prison the Master missed Him very much. He longed to see His Father again. One day a faithful servant who used to live with the Holy Family said he would take the Master to the prison to see Bahá'u'lláh.

They hurried through the dirty streets, stepping over holes and puddles, passing piles of rotting food and rubbish. Flies buzzed around the donkeys, which walked slowly to the market, carrying carpets, cotton, fruit, or corn from the country.

When they arrived at the prison, the servant carried the Master on his shoulders. The warden showed them the way to the cell. They went through a small doorway and down some steps into the darkness. Suddenly they heard the voice of Bahá'u'lláh, saying, "Do not bring Him in here."

The place was too horrible for a little boy. It was very smelly and the prisoners were all chained together in the dark.

The servant carried the Master back up the steps, into the sunlight.

The Prison

The Master and the kind servant who was with Him waited in the prison yard, still hoping to see Bahá'u'lláh.

In the streets nearby, children played and laughed. But the Master was sad as He waited, anxiously watching the little door which led down into the dark prison.

It happened that on that day the prisoners were taken out from the deep dungeon to enjoy the sunshine for a little while. There were many Bábís in the jail then, even though they had done nothing wrong. Eventually, the door opened, and Bahá'u'lláh came slowly out into the daylight. He was chained to another Bábí. The chains were so heavy and Bahá'u'lláh so ill, He could hardly walk.

The Master was horrified at what had happened to His beloved Father. He fainted, and the servant had to carry Him home.

The people who had put Bahá'u'lláh in prison wanted to kill Him. But everyone knew that Bahá'u'lláh had done nothing wrong, and after a few months He was set free.

His enemies still wanted to punish Him, so they told Bahá'u'lláh that He and His family had to go far away and live in another country and never come home again.

The Holy Family went to live in the city of Baghdad, where they stayed for the next ten years.

The Wise Men

The Master was walking with His uncle through the narrow winding streets of Baghdad. The shops were full of interesting things—red, blue, and yellow rugs, pots and pans, parrots, dates, melons, cakes, sweets, and pomegranates. Sometimes there were so many things they overflowed onto the road outside, which was crowded with people, and with donkeys carrying heavy loads.

The Master passed children holding out their hands for a penny, passed the people from the desert riding their milk-white camels, until He came to some wise men sitting in the shade near the mosque talking about God and Muhammad, His Prophet.

The Master often used to talk with these wise men, and they liked to listen to Him. Although He was very young, what He said was wise and true, and He was always gentle and polite.

Once, a nobleman asked Him to write a book explaining some of the difficult things which Muhammad had said. The Master wrote it so well that everyone was amazed when they read it. They asked Him, "Who is your teacher? Where do you learn the things you say?"

The Master replied, "My Father has taught me."

The Mountains

The Master was with His Father all the time. They loved each other very much. But one day Bahá'u'lláh had to go away into the mountains, and He did not come back for two long years.

The Master sometimes cried because He missed His Father so. He read the books of the Báb and prayed. He helped His family as much as He could.

There was an unkind uncle living in their house. He locked the door and would not let the children go out to play. During this sad time, while Bahá'u'lláh was away many of the Bábís in Baghdad forgot the good teachings of the Báb. Some even began to quarrel among themselves.

The Return

One day Bahá'u'lláh returned from the mountains. His clothes were made of rough cloth, His hair and beard were long, and His face was tanned from being so many months outside in the wind and sun. The Master fell to the ground and kissed His Father's feet. Tears fell from Bahá'u'lláh's eyes as He looked at His beloved Son.

After Bahá'u'lláh's return, there was much happiness among the people of Baghdad and many came to visit Him. Some came because they wanted to ask Bahá'u'lláh important questions, and others came just to see what was going on.

Bahá'u'lláh was very busy with all these people, so the Master helped Him. Whenever anyone came to the house, the Master would ask them what they wanted, and if they really wanted to learn the truth, then He would take them to meet Bahá'u'lláh.

Paradise

Bahá'u'lláh, the Master, and a few of the believers were in a boat being rowed across the river Tigris. The Master watched the crowd of waving people on the far-off bank. They seemed to get smaller and smaller as the boat rocked up and down on its journey to the other side.

The sound of voices grew faint and the only sound to be heard was the splash of waves against the boat. Soon they arrived with a bump against the bank on the other side of the river. They got out and went to a beautiful garden.

There were four avenues of trees, and, with the help of some of the friends who had joined them, Bahá'u'lláh's tent was put up in the middle of the garden. It was very windy and the tent swayed. The friends thought it might blow down, so each day and each night they took it in turns to hold the ropes until the wind stopped. This meant they could be close to Bahá'u'lláh, which made them very happy.

The garden was full of sweet-smelling flowers. Each morning the believers made a big pile of roses in Bahá'u'lláh's tent. When the people of Baghdad came to visit Bahá'u'lláh, He would give them some of the roses to take back home. Everyone felt so full of happiness they thought they were in Paradise.

And that is what Bahá'u'lláh called this garden—the Garden of Riḍván, which means the Garden of Paradise.

Bahá'u'lláh stayed twelve days in that lovely garden with the Master and a few friends. The rest of His family came on the ninth day, and on the twelfth day they all left together. They were moving to another city, called Constantinople, which was a very long way away.

But while Bahá'u'lláh was in the Garden of Riḍván, He told His family and friends something very special. Many years before, when the Báb had come with a new message from God, He said that one day God would send another great Messenger, Who would bring love and peace and unity to all the people of the world. It was in the Garden of Riḍván that Bahá'u'lláh told everyone that He was this great Messenger the whole world was waiting for.

From that day forward, the people who believed in Bahá'u'lláh were called Bahá'ís.

The Lamp

A handsome young man on horseback came riding toward the travelers. It was the Master. He had gone ahead to find a place where everyone could camp for the night.

The Holy Family and some of the Bahá'ís had left Baghdad on the first of many journeys that did not end until they arrived at the prison of 'Akká.

These journeys lasted a very long time. Once they had to travel through storms and heavy snow.

One winter they were living in a small house in a city called Adrianople. It was cold and they were all hungry. At night, rats and mice ran through the house. The Master would light a lamp, which would frighten them away, and He would laugh and sing to cheer everyone up.

The Letter

One day the Holy Family were sitting quietly in their house in Adrianople when they heard a bugle call. The Master looked out of the window and saw a ring of soldiers surrounding the house. When He went outside, the soldiers gave Him a letter. It said Bahá'u'lláh was going to be sent away to one place, and the rest of the family to another place. And neither party would know where the other was sent.

The Master said He would rather die than be separated from Bahá'u'lláh. He asked if they could wait a few days, but the soldiers said, "No, you must go today."

The Master said He would like to see the governor in his palace. The family were very worried when they saw Him being led away between two soldiers.

When He saw the governor, the Master asked many times if the family could stay together but the answer was always "No." He went on asking for a whole week and eventually a telegram came that said "Yes."

But although the Holy Family were not parted from each other, they had to leave the town of Adrianople and continue on their long journey, far away from their home in Persia.

Muníb

When Bahá'u'lláh, his family, and friends were being sent from Adrianople to 'Akká, one of the believers became very ill. He was a young man called Muníb. He had just returned from a long visit to Persia, where he had been telling people about Bahá'u'lláh.

Muníb could chant and sing poems very well. He was also very good at doing beautiful writing, and he used to write out the prayers of Bahá'u'lláh. During the night, as Bahá'u'lláh rode along over the desert traveling from one city to another, Muníb and the Master would walk by His side, and Muníb would sing beautiful songs.

But now Muníb was very weak and couldn't even walk. The Bahá'ís had to carry him onto the ship that would take them to 'Akká. However, he became so ill that after a few days the captain said he must go to hospital and he stopped the ship at the next port.

Poor Muníb did not want to leave Bahá'u'lláh, but the captain said that he must. The Master and some of the other friends gently carried him off the ship.

They had only one hour before the ship left again, so they quickly took him to the hospital. The Master kissed him many times and chanted prayers before He had to leave His dear friend Muníb. A little while later Muníb died, and his spirit was free to be with Bahá'u'lláh forever.

Chains

At one time, when the Master was in 'Akká, He was put in chains that the guards locked around His wrists, ankles, and knees. As the guards did this, the Master laughed and sang. Instead of being unhappy, He was so nice to the guards that they soon became His friends, and they tried to help Him whenever they could.

One day He asked to go to the public baths and the guards agreed to take Him. Before leaving, the guards tied the long chains around His waist under His clothes so that no one would see that the Master was a prisoner. However, as they walked through the streets, the chains fell down and people began to mock the Master and crowded around Him, calling Him names.

But the Master did not mind. He held His head high and walked along happily, for He knew that He had done only good things, and that God was pleased with Him.

The Wedding

Back in Persia, a young girl called Munírih Khánum was crying in her bedroom. She was sad because she had heard that Bahá'u'lláh was shut away in a dark prison, far away from the fields and flowers which He loved so much.

Then one day Bahá'u'lláh sent a message to Munírih Khánum, telling her to come with her brother to 'Akká. She was very excited and quickly began getting ready for the long journey.

After many weeks they arrived and every day they were taken to see Bahá'u'lláh. Munírih Khánum also met the Master and sometimes watched from her window as He swam in the sea.

One day Bahá'u'lláh lovingly told her that He had chosen her to be the Master's wife.

On the day of the wedding, Bahá'u'lláh was there with His wife, His daughter, and five other ladies. Munírih Khánum wore a white dress that the Master's mother and sister had made, and on her head was a white veil. She had long, thick plaits and looked very lovely.

Prayers were chanted, and Munírih Khánum and the Master were married.

The Governor

There was a man in 'Akká who was not friendly. He did not like the peaceful, honest Bahá'ís. He thought of a plan to stop them from working, which meant that they would have no money to buy food.

He told the police: "There are fifteen shops owned by Bahá'ís; go tomorrow early, lock them up and bring the keys to me." He was going to keep the keys so that the Bahá'ís could not open their shops!

That evening the Master told the friends not to open their shops the next day, but to wait and see what God would send them.

In 'Akká the shops usually opened at seven o'clock, so early the next morning the governor was waiting for the police to bring him the keys. He waited and waited, but the shops never opened so nobody could get the keys. By ten o'clock the governor was very puzzled and wondered why his plan had not worked.

While he was waiting a man came with a telegram from the government. The telegram said that the governor had lost his job and that the police must take him away at once to another town called Damascus.

The unfriendly governor was very frightened and began to get ready to leave. The Master went to visit him and was very kind. He told him not to worry, and asked if there was anything He could do for him. The governor asked the Master to look after his wife and children after he had gone.

The Master promised that He would. Later He gave them everything they needed to join their father in Damascus, and even sent someone with them to make sure they arrived safely.

It was a long journey, but eventually the governor and his family were all together again. Then the governor was sorry he had been so bad to the Bahá'ís and wrote a letter to the Master that said, "I pray you pardon me, I did not understand. I did not know you!"

Charcoal

The shop was very busy. People came in and out asking questions or leaving messages, and no one took any notice of a man sitting quietly by the door. It was the Master, and He had been waiting for three hours. The shopkeeper had stolen some charcoal which the Bahá'ís in 'Akká had bought for their fires—and the Master had come to get it back.

Eventually the shopkeeper turned to Him and asked, "Are you one of the prisoners in this town?" The Master said He was. Then the shopkeeper asked Him what He had done that He had been sent to prison. The Master said He had only done what Jesus had done—He had told people of a new message from God.

Now the shopkeeper was at first very angry when the Master said this, and rudely asked, "What could you know of Christ?" So the Master politely told him, and when he realized how much the Master knew, the shopkeeper became ashamed of his own bad behavior.

He became a good friend, and paid for all the charcoal he had taken from the Bahá'ís.

The Traveler

Bahá'ís would often walk for months from Persia to visit Bahá'u'lláh in 'Akká, where the Holy Family and friends were imprisoned. The town was surrounded by a thick wall with two locked gates guarded by soldiers.

When the Bahá'ís arrived, tired but happy because they were at last going to see Bahá'u'lláh, they would be stopped at the gate, put in prison for a while, then sent home again. They were not allowed to see Bahá'u'lláh.

One evening the Master, with some of the friends, was walking up and down on a flat roof of one of the houses in 'Akká when He saw a carriage in the distance.

He told them that a holy person was in that carriage. The friends looked but all they could see was a far-off puff of dust by the seashore.

Then the Master said that they should go to the gate. Usually, travelers were not allowed to enter the city, especially if they were suspected of being Bahá'ís, but the Master went to the gate to welcome this visitor just the same.

When He reached the gate, the Master told the guard that a friend was coming and he must let him in. The other friends could not believe their eyes when they saw the guard bring a chair for the Master. And when the carriage arrived, the visitor was allowed in!

The passenger was a very close relative of the Báb and had traveled all the way from India. He was such a good man that as soon as the Master saw the carriage coming, He knew that a pure person was inside.

The Door to Heaven

One day the sad news came that Bahá'u'lláh was ill. His family did all they could to make Him comfortable, but after a few days He died and His Soul left this world to return to God in the world of light.

As the news spread throughout 'Akká, this special prayer was chanted from every mosque in the city:

"God is great.
He giveth life!
He taketh it again!
He dieth not,
But liveth for evermore!"

The prayer could be heard by all the people in the streets, the shops, the houses, and the fields. Hundreds came to say how sad they were and how much they had loved Bahá'u'lláh.

The Master's children also loved Bahá'u'lláh very much. One of them said, "I would like best of all to go to Him. . . . I want to go through that same door to heaven."

The next year this little child became ill and died and went to live with Bahá'u'lláh forever.

At first all the friends felt lost without Bahá'u'lláh to tell them what to do. But then Bahá'u'lláh's Will was read, and in it He said that He had chosen the Master to look after everyone. When we love and obey the Master then we become very close to Bahá'u'lláh too.

Some time after this, the Master said that from now on He would like the friends to call Him *'Abdu'l-Bahá*. 'Abdu'l-Bahá is a very beautiful name which means "Servant of Bahá'u'lláh."

The 'Abá

One day a man who worked for the government came to 'Abdu'l-Bahá and said: "I want an 'abá." An 'abá is a kind of cloak like the ones the Master often wore. 'Abdu'l-Bahá said that He had only one 'abá, which He was wearing, but He would gladly give it to him.

But the man was greedy and very rude. He said he did not like that 'abá but wanted a better one. 'Abdu'l-Bahá said He did not have a better 'abá, but He would give the man some money to buy a good one.

The man went on grumbling so 'Abdu'l-Bahá said He would buy him a new 'abá *and* give him the one He was wearing! But still the man was not happy and said bad things about the Master. He was also bad to other people until, one day, the people in the government became angry with him because of something he had done. They punished him by taking away his job and all his belongings, and in the end he did not have anything.

'Abdu'l-Bahá's Children

One hot afternoon in 'Akká, the children were having tea with 'Abdu'l-Bahá. They were in a cool room with white-washed walls and a blue door. The sun shone through the wide windows onto 'Abdu'l-Bahá's two small grandsons and two little boys from America.

'Abdu'l-Bahá held out His arms, the four children ran toward Him, and He hugged them to His heart. Then they all sat down together. 'Abdu'l-Bahá put sugar in their tea, and stirred it for them, and they all had a very happy time.

'Abdu'l-Bahá was kind to everybody. If people were lonely, He would visit them; if they were hungry, He would take them food; and if they were unhappy, 'Abdu'l-Bahá would make them laugh.

Every day of His life He showed us the right way—how to love God and one another, how to forgive, and how to obey.

'Abdu'l-Bahá loves each one of us and we are all His own special children, even when we grow up.

The Boat

'Abdu'l-Bahá's enemies were planning to put Him in prison again. Some people said He would be sent away to die in a far-off desert. Everyone was worried when they heard this. Even the poor people were too frightened to come to His house for food.

One kind man came to 'Abdu'l-Bahá and told Him that if He got ready quickly, he would take Him away in his boat to a safe place. But 'Abdu'l-Bahá said, "The Báb did not run away, and I shall not run away." He began to mend His house and plant trees in the garden. He even bought enough coal to last through the winter. The people of 'Akká were astonished. But 'Abdu'l-Bahá did not worry, even though spies were hiding outside His house.

One month passed by and then the boat with the people who were going to take 'Abdu'l-Bahá away was seen coming across the bay. Everyone watched as it came closer and closer to the shore. 'Abdu'l-Bahá prayed to God and knew that the right thing would happen in the end.

And it did. Suddenly the boat turned around, sailed away into the open sea, and never came back again!

The Shrine of the Báb

For nearly sixty years after the Báb had been martyred, His sacred body had been kept in hiding so that the enemies of the Faith could not steal it.

Bahá'u'lláh had chosen a spot on the side of Mount Carmel where the Báb should be buried. As soon as He could, 'Abdu'l-Bahá obeyed the command of His Father and began to build the Shrine of the Báb.

At first the owner of the land on the mountain did not want to sell it, so 'Abdu'l-Bahá prayed over and over again a prayer written by the Báb. The next morning the man came to apologize for being so stubborn, and begged 'Abdu'l-Bahá to buy the land from him!

At once 'Abdu'l-Bahá began to build the Shrine. When it was finished, the precious body of the Báb, carefully wrapped in silk, and in a wooden casket, was taken to the Shrine.

It was nighttime and Bahá'ís from the East and from the West gathered on the mountain. By the light of a lamp, 'Abdu'l-Bahá lovingly lowered the wooden casket into one made of beautiful marble. 'Abdu'l-Bahá had taken off His shoes and cloak, and His turban had fallen to the ground. His silver hair waved about His head and His face was shining as He bowed down, laid His forehead on the casket, and prayed.

The Journey

'Abdu'l-Bahá had a little grandson whose name was Shoghi Effendi. He was born when the Holy Family were still prisoners in 'Akká. Then, when they were freed, they moved to Haifa, where the air was fresh and more healthy. Shoghi Effendi spent his time learning prayers, doing lessons, playing with other children, and best of all, being with 'Abdu'l-Bahá as much as he could. They loved each other very much.

One day 'Abdu'l-Bahá decided to take Shoghi Effendi on a great adventure. They were going to America together. 'Abdu'l-Bahá bought him some new clothes and they got ready for the journey.

They traveled by boat from Egypt to Italy, where they had to stop for some passengers to get off, and others to get on. One of the other people traveling with them was jealous of Shoghi Effendi. He made trouble with the doctors in Italy, who said that Shoghi Effendi had something wrong with his eyes and could not go to America.

'Abdu'l-Bahá knew there really was nothing wrong with His grandson. He did everything He could to make the doctors change their minds, but they refused.

Shoghi Effendi had to return to Haifa. 'Abdu'l-Bahá sadly went on His journey to America without him.

The Car

'Abdu'l-Bahá visited America and many other countries. He traveled for thousands of miles, meeting with the friends and giving talks. One of the Bahá'ís wanted to help, and she sent 'Abdu'l-Bahá some money to buy a car so that He could travel more comfortably.

'Abdu'l-Bahá lovingly thanked the lady for this generous gift and praised her for being so kind, but He did not buy a car. He gave back the money and asked her to buy food, clothes, and medicine for the poor people instead.

The Present

The table was full of delicious food and everyone sat down to enjoy a great feast. 'Abdu'l-Bahá was there, passing around the plates piled high with good things to eat. Then one of the friends gave 'Abdu'l-Bahá a present. It had been sent by a very poor man who lived far away, who gave the only thing he had to give—his dinner. It was wrapped up in a clean cotton handkerchief. Inside was a shriveled apple and a piece of dry, black bread.

'Abdu'l-Bahá looked at the present and was very happy. He pushed His plate of food away and He began to eat the old apple and the hard bread. He even broke bits off to share with the friends.

The Poor

It was Christmas time, and the people in London were busy buying presents. But there were some people who did not even have enough money to buy bread for their children.

This made 'Abdu'l-Bahá very sad. He visited many of these poor people, helping them as much as He could.

He told the friends how there were poor people in 'Akká too. The children were often thin and ill. When they asked for a piece of bread, nobody would give them any. Hungry little children, who had not eaten anything all day, would watch people buying bread and rice and cheese from the shops, and wish they could have some too. But the shopkeepers waved their arms and shouted at them to go away.

'Abdu'l-Bahá told the friends that one day in 'Akká some poor people had come to Him begging for food. Nearby was a grocer's shop full of good things to eat. 'Abdu'l-Bahá told them to go to the shop and take whatever they wanted. They rushed to the shop—and were so hungry that they even ate the hard, uncooked rice.

The shopkeeper began to shout and scream that he was being robbed, but no one took any notice. When all the people had gone, and the shop was empty, 'Abdu'l-Bahá paid the shopkeeper for all that had been eaten or taken away.

The Party

It was 'Abdu'l-Bahá's birthday. One of the Bahá'ís wondered what would happen on such an exciting day! She imagined all the presents 'Abdu'l-Bahá would get, and how He'd have the chance to rest for once, while others did the work.

But was she in for a big surprise! When she woke up that morning, her husband told her that 'Abdu'l-Bahá was already in the kitchen, busy baking bread!

Later, two hundred guests came to 'Abdu'l-Bahá's party. He stood all the time, serving them rice, meat, and delicious fruit, and telling them funny stories to make them laugh.

Then He told the friends to forgive each other for any wrong things they might have done, so that everyone would be happy. He said that if we are sad when we eat we become even more sad, but if we are happy when we eat then we become happier.

'Abdu'l-Bahá said that He was not having a party because it was His birthday, but because of something very special which happened the day that He was born. On that day the Báb had told someone for the first time He was the Manifestation of God. And *that* was the reason why 'Abdu'l-Bahá was having a party.

Violets

One day, when 'Abdu'l-Bahá went for a ride in the country with some of the friends, they decided to stop at an inn to have tea. As 'Abdu'l-Bahá stepped out of the car, fifteen small children came running toward Him, each holding bunches of violets that they wanted to sell. They looked up at 'Abdu'l-Bahá, and He looked lovingly down at them—and bought all the violets. Then they held out their hands for more money but 'Abdu'l-Bahá said they already had some, and went into the inn.

Later, when He came out again, there were the children waiting for more money. One of the Bahá'ís sternly told them to go away for they were being greedy. But 'Abdu'l-Bahá noticed a new child, who had not been there before, so He stopped and gave him some pennies too.

The Train

The train was speeding under bridges, over streams and through fields on its way across America. Inside, a crowd of people stood around 'Abdu'l-Bahá.

Some Turkish soldiers came to ask Him questions. 'Abdu'l-Bahá spoke to them and gave them tea. They were going home to fight in a war. This made 'Abdu'l-Bahá very sad. He often said that people should not fight anymore, but should love one another and be friends. He also said that He must leave America and hurry home to the Holy Land so that He could help the poor people who would be hurt and hungry because of this war.

When the soldiers had gone, a man passed by selling pretty glass stones, and children crowded round looking longingly at the lovely colors and wishing they could have some. 'Abdu'l-Bahá told them to choose the stones they liked best. When more children came, 'Abdu'l-Bahá bought stones for them as well.

News of 'Abdu'l-Bahá spread throughout the train. When people heard that such a kind man was in one of the carriages, many came to talk to Him. And 'Abdu'l-Bahá told them about Bahá'u'lláh and His teachings.

The Lonely Stranger

It was very early in the morning and most people were still in bed. One of the Bahá'ís looked out of her bedroom window and saw 'Abdu'l-Bahá in the empty street below.

Suddenly, a poor man passed by. His clothes were thin and torn and very dirty. Maybe he had slept that night on the cold pavement, or under a bridge, and had no one to look after him.

'Abdu'l-Bahá walked up to that lonely old man, held his dirty hand and spoke to him lovingly. The old man was very sad and it took him a long time to cheer up, but eventually he gave a little smile.

Then 'Abdu'l-Bahá looked at the man's ragged trousers, and smiled. He went into a dark porch and took off His own trousers, which He wore underneath His 'abá, and gave them to the old man.

Fred

There was a boy called Fred who was very naughty. His mother told him to be good but he would not listen. He would fight and steal and show off in front of the other boys, and was always in some kind of trouble.

Once when he had been very bad and the police were chasing him down the street, Fred jumped over a high wall and broke his leg.

When Fred was taken to prison, a kind man called Mr. Hall came to see him. Mr. Hall was a lawyer and he worked in the police station. He tried to help Fred and told him about a very wonderful person called 'Abdu'l-Bahá who was visiting America.

Fred listened and thought that he would like to meet 'Abdu'l-Bahá, so Mr. Hall told him where to go. Fred did not have any money, so he climbed on top of trains, and sometimes underneath, and traveled like that for many miles. When he arrived he was dirty and tired. One of the Bahá'ís invited him to stay in her house for the night.

Very early the next morning she woke Fred up and he hurried to meet 'Abdu'l-Bahá. There were a lot of people there and Fred was told to sit down and wait. Fred sat down and sadly thought that it would be a long time before 'Abdu'l-Bahá would want to see him. But soon someone came to tell him 'Abdu'l-Bahá was waiting for him. Fred had a funny feeling inside him as he went up the stairs—he had been very bad, and he wondered if 'Abdu'l-Bahá would be cross with him.

The doors opened, and 'Abdu'l-Bahá smiled at Fred. He took his hands and said, "Welcome! Welcome! Welcome! You are very welcome!"

He asked Fred about his journey, and Fred told Him how he had traveled on top of and underneath trains. 'Abdul-Bahá's eyes shone. He kissed Fred on both cheeks and gave him some fruit. Then he picked up Fred's dirty hat and kissed that too.

Fred stayed with 'Abdu'l-Bahá for a whole week, and he never did anything bad again.

Serving God

In 'Akká, there were many poor people who had no one to look after them except for 'Abdu'l-Bahá. Every winter He bought warm cloaks to give them. Some of the people were blind or hurt. 'Abdu'l-Bahá would gently put their new cloaks around their shoulders and fasten them up.

When people were ill He would help them too, and take food and medicine to their houses.

One day He was very busy, so He asked one of the friends to visit a man who was ill. The Bahá'í was very happy to do this and went at once. But when she went into the sick man's house it was so dirty and there was such a horrible smell that she quickly left and came back to tell 'Abdu'l-Bahá how bad it was.

'Abdu'l-Bahá looked very sad and stern. He said that He had been many times to that house. Couldn't she go just once? If a house was dirty she must clean it, if someone was hungry she must give them food.

If we want to serve God, said 'Abdu'l-Bahá, then we must serve each other.

The World of Light

'Abdu'l-Bahá's hair was now snowy white. His eyes were big and bluey-grey with long, black lashes. His face was very kind and when He looked at you, you felt that He loved you more than anyone else in the world.

That was the way everyone felt when they met 'Abdu'l-Bahá, and that was the way John felt too.

John was a big man who lived in America. Once, when he was alone with 'Abdu'l-Bahá in a car, 'Abdu'l-Bahá had laid His head on John's right shoulder and gone to sleep. John had sat as still as a mouse and did not move until the car stopped.

One day, when 'Abdu'l-Bahá had gone back to live in Haifa, far away from America, He wrote to John and said that He was longing to see him. John hurried to Haifa. But a few days later, 'Abdu'l-Bahá died, and His Soul left this world to be with Bahá'u'lláh in the world of light.

'Abdu'l-Bahá's sister held John's hand and they prayed together for part of that night in the room of 'Abdu'l-Bahá.

Later, John helped carry the coffin up the hill to the Shrine of the Báb. The coffin rested on his right shoulder and he remembered the time, long ago, when 'Abdu'l-Bahá had put His head on his shoulder and gone to sleep.

Glossary

'Abá: A loose, sleeveless, cloak-like outer garment worn by men.

Abbás: 'Abdu'l-Bahá's given name at birth.

'Abdu'l-Bahá: The title assumed by Abbás Effendi (1844–1921), the eldest son and successor of Bahá'u'lláh and the Center of His Covenant; translates to: *Servant of Bahá.*

Adrianople: Present-day Edirne, a city in European Turkey to which Bahá'u'lláh and His family were exiled in 1863, and where they resided for five years.

'Akká: *Acre, Akko;* A four-thousand-year-old seaport and prison-city in northern Israel surrounded by fortress-like walls facing the sea. In 1868 Bahá'u'lláh and His family and companions were banished to 'Akká. Bahá'u'lláh named 'Akká "the Most Great Prison."

Bábí: Follower of the Báb or pertaining to His Faith.

Baghdad: Capital city in modern-day Iraq, situated along the Tigris River, where the Holy Family lived for ten years.

Bahá'u'lláh: *The Glory of God;* title of Mírzá Husayn-'Alí (12 November 1817–29 May 1892), Founder of the Bahá'í Faith. Bahá'ís refer to Him by a variety of titles, including the Promised One of All Ages, the Blessed Beauty, the Blessed Perfection, and the Ancient Beauty.

Constantinople: The old name for the city of Istanbul, in the modern-day country of Turkey.

Damascus: Capital city of Syria.

Haifa: Seaport in northern Israel where the Bahá'í World Center is located.

Holy Family: Generally, Bahá'ís use this term to refer to the family of Bahá'u'lláh.

Kalím: Also known as *Áqáy-i-Kalím.* A younger full brother of Bahá'u'lláh who recognized the station of the Báb and of Bahá'u'lláh and faithfully served Bahá'u'lláh throughout His exiles. He often met with government officials and religious leaders on Bahá'u'lláh's behalf until 'Abdu'l-Bahá assumed that function.

Manifestation of God: Designation of a Prophet Who is the Founder of a religious Dispensation.

Master, The: A title of 'Abdu'l-Bahá referring to the virtues He manifested and to His role as an enduring model for humanity to emulate.

Mosque: a Muslim temple or place of public worship.

Munírih Khánum: *Illumined;* the name bestowed on Fátimih Khánum, who came to 'Akká at Bahá'u'lláh's invitation to marry 'Abdu'l-Bahá in 1873.

Nabíl: The title of Muhammad-i-Zarandí, a devoted follower of the Báb and Bahá'u'lláh, and author of the historical work known as "Nabíl's Narrative."

Navváb: *Most Exalted Leaf;* Wife of Bahá'u'lláh and mother of 'Abdu'l-Bahá, Bahíyyih Khánum, and Mírzá Mihdí. She married Bahá'u'lláh in 1835, accompanied Him in His exiles, and died in 1886. Bahá'u'lláh named her His "perpetual consort in all the worlds of God."

Persia: Historic region of southwestern Asia associated with the area that is now modern Iran. The people of that region have traditionally called their country Iran, and the name was officially adopted in 1935.

Public baths: Public bathing facilities that originated from a communal need for cleanliness at a time when most people did not have access to private bathing facilities.

Ridván: *Paradise;* Name given by Bahá'u'lláh to the Garden of Najíbíyyih in Baghdad, where He publicly declared His mission in April 1863.

Shoghi Effendi: The title by which Shoghi Rabbání (1897–1957), great-grandson of Bahá'u'lláh, is known to Bahá'ís. He was appointed Guardian of the Bahá'í Faith and authorized interpreter of Bahá'u'lláh's and 'Abdu'l-Bahá's writings.

Shrine: Refers to the burial places of Bahá'u'lláh, the Báb, and 'Abdu'l-Bahá.

Tigris River: The second largest river in western Asia. With the Euphrates, it makes up a river system that borders the area known as the Fertile Crescent. An important source of both travel and irrigation, the Tigris also has a rich history that dates back to the earliest known civilizations.

Warden: The chief administrative officer in charge of a prison.

World of Light: Sometimes referred to as the Abhá Kingdom, *the Most Glorious Kingdom,* the spiritual world beyond this world.

References

The Master. See H. M. Balyuzi, *'Abdu'l-Bahá* (Oxford: George Ronald, 1971).

School. Nabíl-i-A'zam, *The Dawn-Breakers,* p. 441 (Wilmette, IL: Bahá'í Publishing Trust, 1999).

The Sheep. *Star of the West,* Vol. XIII, no. 10, Jan 1923, pp. 271–72.

Illness. H. M. Balyuzi, *'Abdu'l-Bahá,* pp. 12–13.

Hunger. Ibid., p. 9.

The Chase. Ibid., p. 10.

The Money. Ibid.

The Gang. Nabíl-i-A'zam, *The Dawn-Breakers,* p. 616.

A Terrible Place. H. M. Balyuzi, *'Abdu'l-Bahá,* pp. 11–12.

The Prison. Ibid.

The Wise Men. Ibid., pp. 13–14.

The Mountains. Ibid., p. 14; Shoghi Effendi, *God Passes By,* pp. 186–97.

The Return. Sarah Louisa Blomfield, *The Chosen Highway,* pp. 51–53 (Wilmette, IL: Bahá'í Publishing Trust, 1967).

Paradise. H. M. Balyuzi, *'Abdu'l-Bahá,* p. 13.

The Lamp. Ibid., p. 17.

The Letter. Myron H. Phelps, *The Master in 'Akká,* pp. 64–65 (Los Angeles: Kalimat Press, 1985).

Muníb. 'Abdu'l-Bahá, *Memorials of the Faithful,* no. 56 (Wilmette, IL: Bahá'í Publishing Trust, 1997).

Chains. Marzieh Gail, *The Sheltering Branch,* pp. 99–100 (Oxford: George Ronald, 1959).

The Wedding. Sarah Louisa Blomfield, *The Chosen Highway,* pp. 87–88.

The Governor. Ibid., pp. 137–39.

Charcoal. H. M. Balyuzi, *'Abdu'l-Bahá,* pp. 33–34.

The Traveler. 'Abdu'l-Bahá, *Memorials of the Faithful,* no. 50.

The 'Abá. Sarah Louisa Blomfield, *The Chosen Highway,* p. 143.

The Governor. Ibid., pp. 103, 106, 137–39.

The Door to Heaven. Sarah Louisa Blomfield, *The Chosen Highway,* ch. 4.

'Abdu'l-Bahá's Children. Juliet Thompson, *The Diary of Juliet Thomson,* p. 40 (Los Angeles: Kalimat Press, 1983); *World Order Magazine,* Fall 1971, p. 51.

The Boat. H. M. Balyuzi, *'Abdu'l-Bahá,* pp. 118–21.

The Shrine of the Báb. Shoghi Effendi, *God Passes By,* pp. 436–37.

The Journey. Ruhíyyih Khánum, *The Priceless Pearl,* pp. 19–20 (London: Bahá'í Publishing Trust, 2017).

The Car. Sarah Louisa Blomfield, *The Chosen Highway,* pp. 157, 159.

The Present. Ibid., pp. 157, 161.

The Poor. H. M. Balyuzi, *'Abdu'l-Bahá,* pp. 351–52.

The Party. Marzieh Gail, *The Sheltering Branch,* pp. 69–71.

Violets. Juliet Thompson, *The Diary of Juliet Thomson,* pp. 175–76; *World Order Magazine,* Fall 1971, p. 55.

The Train. H. M. Balyuzi, *'Abdu'l-Bahá,* pp. 309, 316.

The Lonely Stranger. Howard Colby Ives, *Portals to Freedom,* p. 129.

Fred. H. M. Balyuzi, *'Abdu'l-Bahá,* pp. 247–50.

Serving God. Ibid., p. 196; Howard Colby Ives, *Portals to Freedom,* p. 85.

The World of Light. *World Order Magazine,* Fall 1971, pp. 38, 41, 44.